RAPS &
RHYMES

★★★★★★★★★★★★★★★★★★★★★★★★★★★★★★★

Susan Hill

ELEANOR CURTAIN
PUBLISHING

First published in Australia in 1990
Reprinted 1990, 1991, 1992, 1994
ELEANOR CURTAIN PUBLISHING
906 Malvern Road
Armadale 3143

The National Library of Australia
Cataloguing In Publication Data
Hill, Susan (Susan Elizabeth).
Raps and rhymes.

ISBN 1 875327 037
(1). Nursery rhymes, English — Study and
teaching (Primary). (2). Children's poetry.
English — Study and teaching (Primary).
I. Title.

372 54044

Produced by Sylvana Scannapiego,
Island Graphics
Designed by Sharon Carr
Illustrated by Cam Knuckey
Edited by Heather Kelly
Typeset by Trade Graphics Pty Ltd
Printed by Impact Printing (Vic) Pty Ltd

Contents

Action rhymes

Two-part reading

Shared reading of many parts

Nonsense

Further reading

Acknowledgements

Thanks to teachers and children: Chris Hastwell and Sue Brock at East Adelaide Primary School, Jane O'Loughlin at Mercedes College, teachers at St. Bernadettes, and students: Mary Sofis, Mary Shannon, Dianne Barrett, Kim Turner, James Andrews, Peter Jarvis and Gaynor Herrman for the Horathe arrangement and Wendy Parson S.A.C.A.E.

The author and publisher thank the following copyright holders for permission to reprint material in this book. If any errors in acknowledgements have occurred they were inadvertent and will be corrected in subsequent editions as they are brought to our notice.

'Ranky tank', 'Little Sally Walker', 'Pretty pear tree' and 'Put your finger on your head' are reproduced by kind permission of Essex Music Australia Pty Limited; 'Put your shoes on' and 'Father says' are reproduced by kind permission of Andre Deutsch Ltd. 'Billy Batter' and 'Alligator Pie' by Dennis Lee are from *Alligator Pie* by Dennis Lee, published by Macmillan of Canada, © 1974, Dennis Lee, and 'I eat kids yum yum' by Dennis Lee is from *Garbage Delight* by Dennis Lee, published by Macmillan of Canada, © 1977. We acknowledge Polygram for the use of 'Hambone', Doubleday and Co. Inc. for 'Song of the popcorn', Holt, Rinehart and Winston Inc. for 'Three little fishes' and Happy Valley Music for 'The old lady from Brewster'.

Introduction

Reading aloud as a group, joining in with a chant or a rhyme, is a great warm up to any lesson and a good way of building up a feeling of cohesiveness in the classroom. The raps and rhymes in this collection can be read aloud and modified in many ways. They have already been read, played with and changed by children from 5 to 12 years of age.

We all love stamping, chanting and clapping to a beat. We also like to change the words around and improvise, adding a clap here, a new word there, to suit how we feel on the day. While most of these chants have been arranged with ideas for performance, the suggestions should be modified to suit the group.

Raps are a form of rhythmic chant too. They are also known as street rhymes or hip hops and are related to jazz vocalization where a lead voice sets up a rhythm and another voice or a group voice improvises or repeats the words of the lead voice. Lots of these raps can be traced back to the group polyphony heard in African music where a lead voice and a group voice are combined in various ways to compliment a rhythm. But not all these chants and raps can be traced to Africa. Many of these rhymes are heard on the street corners and playgrounds of Australia, Britain and the United States.

You may have heard versions of these rhymes before because chants, raps and street rhymes are often improvised by different groups as they learn them. Sometimes the chants are improvised by changing the rhythm and sometimes the rhyme is changed. Once children are introduced to the chants they quickly find the beat or clapping pattern and in no time have invented versions of their own.

In her collection of games and chants from Afro-American heritage, *Step it down*, Bessie Jones says about group chants and rhymes: 'Enjoy yourself. This is a beautiful democratic tradition, full of joy and the juices of life. Don't be too solemn, or too organized these are for play.'

Getting the rhythm

To get the beat, try clapping 1, 2, 3, 4 to the chants. Most chants will fit this straightforward beat. Then try clicking your fingers to one or two lines, then alternate with claps. There are some suggestions about where to clap or click or do actions on the page alongside the chants. As the key idea is to have fun and improvise, these suggestions could be used on an initial run-through then the children's ideas could be sought and followed.

Standing up as you read and chant is a good idea. This allows footstamping and weight transference. Bessie Jones does a footstamp movement where the left foot slides forward with the weight still on the right foot, then the weight is transferred to the left foot as the right foot steps forward. Hands clap in time and at the same side as the foot sliding forward.

Trying it is the only way!!! After several attempts and lots of laughs you'll get it and know you've got it because it feels right.

Getting the volume and pitch

Try clapping, then clicking, then stamping to the chants and you'll notice the pitch and volume changes. If I clap my thighs I get a different sound from clapping the back of my hand. Claps can sound high and sharp when hands are stretched tight, or deep and mellow when hands are cupped. Variations of clapping, clicking and slapping are known as hand jiving. A good example of a hand jive is found in 'Hambone'.

Fast clapping

Some of the chants are clapping games where partners learn a chant then clap their own and a partner's hands. Bessie Jones introduces this pattern which can be fitted to lots of chants:

O Players clap their own hands
R Players clap right hands
L Players clap left hands
X Players clap both hands together

Try this:

O		R	O	L	O	R	O	L	X
	Green	Sally	up		Green	Sally	down		
O		R	O	L	O	R	O	L	X
	Green	Sally	bake		her	possum	brown		

Now try clapping this rhyme and try to get faster:

I asked my mama for fifteen cents
To see the elephant jump the fence
He jumped so high he touched the sky
And didn't get back till the fourth of July.

Reading the raps and rhymes

The best way for everyone to read the rhymes and chants is to write them out on butcher's paper. The whole class should be able to see the words. The teacher can point to each word in much the same way as big books are read.

Silent reading and reading aloud

Silent reading by the class as the teacher reads aloud is the best preparation for performing the chants. Like adults, children don't like to be put on the spot by being asked to read aloud when they haven't read it through silently first. Round Robin reading without preparation is to be discouraged.

Assigning readers

Readers can be selected according to their ability, but putting a proficient reader with someone who needs more practice also works well. Many of the chants have group voices, some have cumulative voices as readers are added one by one. Improvision is up to you!

Improvise, improvise . . .

When the children come up with ideas for performing the raps, chants or rhymes their ideas are usually more ingenious than any adults' ideas. Anyone who doubts this should watch the complex chanting and clapping games played outside the classroom. So enjoy yourself . . . have fun . . . there is no real sequence to follow from easy to difficult. Read the chants and choose those you like. There are clapping chants, chants for two voices, raps for many voices and rhymes that can be performed as Readers Theatre.

Susan Hill

Improvising

Army song

Remember this old army song? It was sung on long marches to keep the troops alert. Improvise by adding a new sentence after 'I don't know but I've been told'.

Leader	**I don't know but I've been told**
Group	**I don't know but I've been told**
Leader	**Adelaide streets are made of gold**
Group	**Adelaide streets are made of gold**
Leader	**Sound off**
Group	**Sound off**
Leader	**1 2 3 4**
Group	**1-2 3-4**

Raps

Raps are improvised chants with an underlying rhythm, for example the rhythm could be a 1,2,3,4 beat. Sometimes raps have an internal rhyme and sometimes the final word on each line rhymes. A quick and easy rap to try out your improvising skills is as follows:

Leader	**Grandma went to the corner store**			
Group	1	2	3	4
Leader	**Grandpa went to the corner store**			
Group	1	2	3	4

(Improvise ....for several lines)

Leader	**All went down to the corner store**			
Group	1	2	3	4
Leader	**They haven't been seen no more**			
Group	1	2	3	4

Hey Johnny!

Children sit in a circle and click fingers or slap thighs to a 1,2,3,4 beat then the group joins in reading the chant. At the end of the rhyme a child is chosen to clap, slap or click a rhythm. It works best if four actions are done in time with the 4/4 beat. Everyone watches the actions carefully then the child who has completed the actions nominates someone to copy his or her rhythm. This nominated child does the actions and then leads off the new set of actions at the end of the rhyme next time it is chanted.

Hey Johnny do you want to be bright?
Meet you on the corner on Saturday night.
You can wiggle you can wobble
You can do the twist,
But I bet you, I bet you.
You can't do this.

(Now do a series of actions in time with four claps)

*Claps or clicks occur on every beat. As children become more confident variations of body claps, vocal sounds and slaps can be introduced. Children may click fingers, slap thighs, make vocal sound, clap hands or put their hands on their head. In these more complex routines everyone has to watch carefully to make sure the child copying is accurate.

I came to the river

Children clap in 4/4 time. This rhyme comes from North American folklore. As it is very predictable the missing words encourage the children to continue it on their own. The rhyme can be added to as children become confident about improvising.

I came to the river but I couldn't get across,
I jumped on a frog 'cause I thought he was a log,
The log wouldn't float so I traded for a goat,
The goat wouldn't holler so I sold him for a dollar,
The dollar wouldn't spin so I threw him in the bin,
The bin wouldn't close so I traded for a rose,
The rose wouldn't pull so I traded for a bull,
The bull wouldn't roar so I threw him out the door,
The .... shut .... hut,
.... stand .... band,
.... play .... hay,
.... OK .... thought I'd stay.

Claps and clicks

★★

Hell, hell

This clapping or thigh-slapping game is played with children sitting in a circle. The children name off and number off around the circle, 'Hell, Matthew, Mark, John, 1, 2, 3, 4, 5, 6, 7, 8, 9, ... 20'. These names and numbers are also written on the blackboard so children remember who is playing the game.

Hell	1	5	9	13
Matthew	2	6	10	14
Mark	3	7	11	15
John	4	8	12	16

The children begin clapping in the 1,2,3,4 time. Hell begins at the count of 4 by saying: 'Hell, hell, 9,9'. Then the child numbered off at 9 says: '9,9, Mark, Mark'. Then Mark answers with his name first: 'Mark, Mark, 11,11', and so on.

It is important that the 4/4 beat is retained. If a player misses a beat their name or number is erased from the blackboard. They can be assigned a new name or number rather than going out. If children do not go out they continue playing and this makes the game non-competitive. You will have to set a time limit as children rarely want to stop.

The following raps and rhymes have an underlying 4/4 beat. The rhythm can be kept by clapping, finger clicking, thigh slapping or foot stamping.

Three bears

Once upon a time
In a nursery rhyme
There were three bears   *   *   *
A momma and a poppa
And a wee bear.   *   *   *

One day they went a walking
And a talking in the woods.
Along came a girl
With a long golden curl.

There were three bears   *   *   *
A momma and a poppa
And a wee bear   *   *   *

'Someone has stolen my porridge',
said the poppa bear.
'Someone has stolen my porridge',
said the momma bear.
'Hey momma three bear',
said the little wee bear,
'Someone has eaten my share, YEH!'

Goldilocks woke up

And broke up the party.
(Wave hands)

'Bye bye, bye bye, bye bye',
said the poppa bear.
'Bye bye, bye bye, bye bye',
said the momma bear.
(Click fingers)

'Hey momma three bear',

said the little wee bear.
'Someone has broken my chair, YEH!'

*	finger click
•	clap
👍	thumbs up on YEH

Queen Nefertiti

This is a cumulative rhyme where more and more readers join in. Assign children as readers 1–19. Ask all class members to clap the 4/4 beat and all come in on the final line.

Reader 1	Spin a coin, spin a coin,
Readers 1 and 2	All fall down;
Readers 1 to 3	Queen Nefertiti
Readers 1 to 4	Stalks through the town.
Readers 1 to 5	Over the pavements
Readers 1 to 6	Her feet go clack.
Readers 1 to 7	Her legs are as tall
Readers 1 to 8	As a chimney stack;
Readers 1 to 9	Her fingers flicker
Readers 1 to 10	Like snakes in the air,
Readers 1 to 11	The walls split open
Readers 1 to 12	At her green-eyed stare:
Readers 1 to 13	Her voice is thin
Readers 1 to 14	As the ghost of bees:
Readers 1 to 15	She will crumble your bones.
Readers 1 to 16	She will make your blood freeze.
Readers 1 to 17	Spin a coin, spin a coin,
Readers 1 to 18	All fall down:
Readers 1 to 19	Queen Nefertiti
All	Stalks through the town.

Hambone

This chant has a hand jive called the Hambone Pat to accompany it. The Hambone Pat occurs at the end of each line. It is made up of:

1. Slap the side of your thigh with the palm of your hand in an upwards movement.
2. Continuing the upwards movement pat your chest.
3. Strike the thighs downwards with the back of your hand.
4. Quickly strike your thighs three times.

Begin by patting both thighs on the off beat underlined in the first lines.

Ham<u>bone</u>, Ham<u>bone</u>, pat <u>him</u> on the shou<u>lder</u>
If you <u>get</u> a pretty <u>girl</u>, I'll show you <u>how</u> to hold <u>her</u>.
Ham<u>bone</u>, Ham<u>bone</u>, where <u>have</u> you <u>been</u>?
All '<u>round</u> the <u>world</u> and <u>back</u> ag<u>ain</u>.
Hambone, Hambone, what did you do?
I got a train and I fairly flew.
Hambone, Hambone, where did you go?
I hopped up to Miss Lucy's door.
I asked Miss Lucy would she marry me.
(in falsetto)'Well, I don't care if Papa don't care!'
First came in was Mister Snake,
He crawled all over that wedding cake.
Next walked in was Mister Tick,
He ate so much that it made him sick.
Next walked in was Mister Coon,
We asked him to sing us a wedding tune.
Now Ham...
Now Ham...

My mother works

Reader 1   **My mother works**
At a pastry shop

All   **Yum, yum**
(Pause)
Yum, Yum

Reader 2   **My father works**
In the orchestra

All   **Twiddle le dee**
Twiddle le dum,
Yum, yum
(Pause)
Yum, yum.

Reader 3	My grandfather works At the rubbish dump Phew ee! Twiddle le dee Twiddle le dum ...
Reader 4	My grandmother works At the telephone exchange
All	Hello, hello ... What's your name? Goodbye! Phew ee! ...
Reader 5	My uncle works At the cowboy shop
All	Bang, bang. You're dead 60 bullets of lead Hello, hello ...? (Continue)

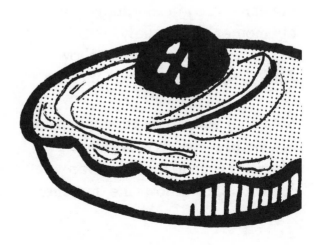

Clapping song

This is a partner clapping game. Children in pairs face each other.
X = clap hands, L = clap left hands, R = clap right hands, O = clap both partner's hands.

X L X R   X O O O (repeat on each line)

My father comes from Germany
My mother comes from Italy
My sister comes from a disco show
And the baby follows me, me, me.

My father works at the ABC
My mother works at the bakery
My sister works at the disco show
And the baby follows me, me, me.

My father likes to smoke his pipe
My mother likes to read her book
My sister likes to show her knee
And the baby follows me, me, me.

My father died in Germany
My mother died in Italy
My sister died at the disco show
And the baby follows me, me, me.

My father went to Germany heaven
My mother went to Italy heaven
My sister went to disco heaven
And the baby follows me, me, me.

Swapping song

Children clap the beat in a 4/4 time. All join in on the chorus while groups of readers read alternate verses.

Refrain

* * *   *
To my wing wong waddle!
* * *   *
To my jack straw straddle

And Johnny's got his fiddle

And he's gone on home.

Group 1   My father died but I don't know how:
          He left me a horse to hitch to the plough.   (Refrain)
Group 2   I swapped my horse and got me a cow,
          And in that trade I just learned how.   (Refrain)
Group 3   I swapped my cow and got me a calf,
          And in that trade I lost just half.   (Refrain)
Group 4   I swapped my calf and got me a pig,
          The poor little thing it never grew big.   (Refrain)
Group 5   I swapped my pig and got me a hen
          To lay me an egg every now and then.   (Refrain)
Group 6   I swapped my hen and got me a cat,
          The pretty little thing by the chimney sat.   (Refrain)
Group 7   I swapped my cat and got me a mouse,
          His tail caught a-fire and he burned down the
          house.   (Refrain)
Group 8   I swapped my mouse and got me a mole,
          The dad-burned thing went straight down its
          hole.   (Refrain)

Ronald McDonald

This is a partner game.
1. Partners face each other.
2. Hold right hands palm up and left hands palm down. *
3. Clap partner's hands this way twice.
4. Hold hands upright and clap partner's twice. •
5. On the words 'a biscuit' point thumbs over your shoulders.
Repeat this pattern for lines 1–6.
Lines 7–8, point thumbs down for the last phrase.
Line 9, imitate a roller coaster for the last phrase.
Line 10, hug yourself on the last phrase.
Line 11, thrust fist forward on the last phrase.

Ronald McDonald 'a biscuit'   (Thumbs up)

Ronald McDonald 'a biscuit'   (Thumbs up)

Oh shoo, shoo, wow, wow, 'a biscuit'   (Thumbs up)

I've got a boy/girl friend, 'a biscuit'   (Thumbs up)

He/She so sweet, 'a biscuit'   (Thumbs up)

Sweeter than a cherry treat, 'a biscuit'   (Thumbs up)

Ice-cream soda with a cherry, 'on the top'   (Thumbs down)

Ice-cream soda with a cherry, 'on the top'   (Thumbs down)

Down baby down by the, 'roller coaster'   (Hands like coaster)

Sweet, sweet baby I don't want to, 'let you go'   (Hug yourself)

Shimmy, shimmy coco pop, 'shimmy, shimmy, pow'   (Thrust fist)

Shimmy, shimmy coco pop, 'shimmy, shimmy, pow'   (Thrust fist)

Old Farmer Joe

There are many versions of this rhyme. It is a clapping chant done in pairs. Children face each other and clap the following pattern.

T O R O L O R O X
(Continue this pattern on every line)

Old farmer Joe, Joe, Joe.
Had one brown cow, cow, cow.
That loved to graze, graze, graze.
On fresh green grass, grass, grass.

Old farmer Joe, Joe, Joe.
Had two fat pigs, pigs, pigs.
Who loved to roll, roll, roll
In the slushy mud, mud, mud.

Old farmer Joe, Joe, Joe.
Had three woolly sheep, sheep, sheep
Who wanted to eat, eat, eat.
Until they sleep, sleep, sleep.

Old farmer Joe, Joe, Joe
Had four noisy ducks, ducks, ducks
That always quack, quack, quack.
All through the night, night, night.

Old farmer Joe, Joe, Joe.
Had one brown cow, cow, cow
And two fat pigs, pigs, pigs
And three woolly sheep, sheep, sheep.
And four noisy ducks, ducks, ducks
That always quack, quack, quack.
All through the night, night, night.

Old farmer Joe, Joe, Joe
Don't work too hard, hard, hard
You need some rest, rest, rest
And time to sleep, sleep, sleep.

Miss Mary Mac, Mac, Mac

Miss Mary Mac, Mac, Mac
All dressed in black, black, black
With silver buttons, buttons, buttons
All down her back, back, back.
She cannot read, read, read
She cannot write, write, write
But she can smoke, smoke, smoke
Her father's pipe, pipe, pipe.

She asked her mother, mother, mother
For fifty cents, cents, cents
To see the elephant, elephant, elephant
Climb up the fence, fence, fence
He climbed so high, high, high
He reached the sky, sky, sky
And never came back, back, back
Till the fourth of July, ly, ly.
She went upstairs, stairs, stairs
And bumped her head, head, head
And now she's DEAD.

Miss Mary Mac, Mac, Mac
(Another version)

Miss Mary Mac, Mac, Mac
All dressed in black, black, black
With silver buttons, buttons, buttons
All down her back, back, back.
Miss Betty Bean, Bean, Bean
All dressed in green, green, green
She never smiled, smiled, smiled
She was too mean, mean, mean.
Miss Lucy Light, Light, Light
All dressed in white, white, white
She kicked her brother, brother, brother
Just out of spite, spite, spite.
Miss Dora Down, Down, Down
All dressed in brown, brown, brown
She pinched her sister, sister, sister
Just to make her frown, frown, frown.

Miss Flora Fay, Fay, Fay
All dressed in gray, gray, gray
Had mumps and measles, measles, measles
On a single day, day, day.
There's soda crackers, crackers, crackers
Up on the shelf, shelf, shelf
If you want any more, more, more
You can sing it yourself, self, self.

Mammy's little baby

Songs can work well as chants. Try different kinds of expressions when reading these. Vary the volume and the pace.

(Chorus)
Mammy's little baby loves short'nin', short'nin'
Mammy's little baby loves short'nin' bread.

Mammy's little baby loves short'nin', short'nin',
Mammy's little baby loves short'nin' bread.

Three little fellers lyin' in bed;
Two was sick and the other 'most dead.
Send for the doctor, the doctor said,
'Feed them babies — short'nin' bread'. *(Chorus)*

Slipped in the kitchen, slip up the lid
Slipped my pockets full of short'nin' bread.
Stole the skillet, stole the lid,
Stole the gal to make me short'nin' bread. *(Chorus)*

They caught me with the skillet, they caught me with the lid
They caught me with the girl making short'nin' bread.
Paid six dollars for the skillet, paid six dollars for the lid,
Spent six months in jail eating short'nin' bread! *(Chorus)*

The song of the popcorn

Pop-pop-pop!
Says the popcorn in the pan
Pop-pop-pop!
You may catch us if you can!
Pop-pop-pop!
Says each kernel hard and yellow;
Pop-pop-pop!
I'm a dancing little fellow.
Pop-pop-pop!
How I scamper through the heat!
Pop-pop-pop!
You will find me good to eat.
Pop-pop-pop!
I can whirl and skip and hop.
Pop-pop-pop-pop-pop, pop, POP!

Action Rhymes

Doctor Knickerbocker

Doctor Knickerbocker, Knickerbocker, number nine
Loves to dance to the rhythm of time.

Now let's get the rhythm of the hands
(Clap, clap)
Now we've got the rhythm of the hands
(Clap, clap)
Now let's get the rhythm of the feet
(Stamp, stamp)
Now we've got the rhythm of the feet
(Stamp, stamp)
Now let's get the rhythm of the eyes
(Rub finger across eyebrow)
Now we've got the rhythm of the eyes
(Rub finger across eyebrow)
Now let's get the rhythm of the dance
(Wiggle bottom)
Now we've got the rhythm of the dance
(Wiggle bottom)
Now let's get the rhythm of the number nine
One, two, three, four, five, six, seven, eight, nine.

(Repeat the rhyme)

I had a little brother

This chant works well when children chosen to be the doctor, the nurse and the lady walk in or out when called. A child, Tiny Tim, could mime actions out the front.

Reader 1	**I had a little brother**
All	**His name was Tiny Tim**
Reader 2	**I put him in the bathtub**
All	**To teach him how to swim.**
Reader 3	**He drank up all the water**
All	**He ate up all the soap,**
Reader 4	**He died last night**
All	**With a bubble in his throat**
Reader 5	**In came the doctor** (Walks in)
Reader 6	**In came the nurse** (Walks in)
Reader 7	**In came the lady** (Walks in)
All	**With the alligator purse.**
Reader 5	**DEAD said the doctor** (All read the words except 'dead'.)
Reader 6	**DEAD said the nurse**
Reader 7	**DEAD said the lady**
All	**With the alligator purse.**
Reader 5	**Out went the doctor** (Walks out)
Reader 6	**Out went the nurse** (Walks out)
Reader 7	**Out went the lady** (Walks out)
All	**With the alligator purse.**
Reader 1	**But then my little brother**
All	**Whose name was Tiny Tim**
Reader 2	**Sat upon his little bed**
All	**And gave a mighty grin.**

Reader 3	He ate up all his dinner,
All	He drank up all his drink,
Reader 4	He laughed and laughed
All	Until he cried, and then —
	What do you think?

Reader 5	In came the doctor (Walks in)
Reader 6	In came the nurse (Walks in)
Reader 7	In came the lady (Walks in)
All	With the alligator purse.

Reader 5	GOOD said the doctor
Reader 6	GOOD said the nurse
Reader 7	GOOD said the lady
All	With the alligator purse.

Reader 5	Out went the doctor (Walks out)
Reader 6	Out went the nurse (Walks out)
Reader 7	Out went the lady (Walks out)
All	With the alligator purse.

The old lady from Brewster

There's an old lady from Brewster   (Clap to the beat)
She had two hens   (Hold up two fingers)
and a rooster   (Hold up one finger)
The rooster died   (Cross hands over your
                        chest)

the old hen cried   (Put your hands over your
                        face)

I can't lay eggs like I used to   (Shake your head)
Now Ma you look so   (Search for hens, hands
                        over eyes)

Now Pa you look so   (Search for hens, hands
                        over eyes)

He said 'Who's been here since I been gone?'
'Two little boys with the red cap on!'   (Hold up two fingers and
                        tap your head)

Hang them boys on a hickory stick
Papa's gonna parch them soon! Wham!

Pain in the head!   Ranky Tanky
Pain in the shoulder!   Ranky Tanky
Pain in the waist!   Ranky Tanky
Pain in the thigh!   Ranky Tanky
Pain in the knee!   Ranky Tanky
Pain in the leg!   Ranky Tanky
Pain in the feet!   Ranky Tanky
Pains all over me!   Ranky Tanky

Children touch parts of the body where the pain is mentioned.

Nicky, knacky, knocky, noo

Touch parts of the body as they are called. Individual readers can read each verse and all join in on the chorus.

Individual reader
With my hands on my head,
What have we here?
This is my main thinker,
My teacher dear.
Chorus
Main thinker,
Nicky, knacky, knocky, noo
That's what they taught me
When I went to school.

Individual reader
With my hands on my head,
What have we here?
These are my eye blinkers,
My teacher dear.
Chorus
Main thinker, eye blinkers
Nicky, knacky, knocky, noo
That's what they taught me
When I went to school.

This is my smell boxer.
This is my chin wagger.
This is my cough chester.
This is my bread basket.
These are my knee knockers.
These are my toe tappers.

Music makers

My auntie plays the piccolo,
My uncle plays the flute,
They practise every night at ten,
Tweetly tweet **TOOT-TOOT!**

My granny plays the banjo,
My grandad plays the drum,
They practise every night at nine,
Plankety plank **BUMM-BUMM!!**

My sister plays the tuba,
My brother plays the guitar,
They practise every night at six,
Twankity **OOM-PA-PA!!!!**

My mother plays the mouth organ,
My daddy plays the oboe,
They practise every night at eight,
Pompity-pom suck blow!!!!!!!!

Ranky tank

This chant was found in Bessie Jones' book, *Step it down*. Bessie Jones says 'Ranky tank' can be improvised in many ways by the lead voice calling out short sentences and the group chanting 'Ranky tank'.

Clap the chant through first. Once the rhyme has been practised the children can learn to 'moonwalk', which is a form of rap dancing.

Moonwalking is a stepping dance where the weight is kept on one foot while the other foot pushes the dancer along, very much like the action of a child riding a scooter.

Moonwalking looks like walking on the spot but small movement forward does occur. Children can moonwalk in a large circle as they chant Ranky tank. If you can't moonwalk, ask a child to teach you.

Lead voice	*Group voice*
Oh ranky tank,	Ranky tank
Oh, ranky tank,	Ranky tank
Papa's goin' to rank	Ranky tank
Mama's goin' to rank	Ranky tank
Down in the cornfield	Ranky tank
I'm goin' to rank,	Ranky tank
Sun is hot,	Ranky tank
See me a-rankin'	Ranky tank
Oh, ranky tank,	Ranky tank
Oh, ranky tank.	Ranky tank

Put your finger on your head

Divide the class into two groups. One group reads the plain type and the other the **bold** type.

Put your finger on your head, **on your head,**
Put your finger on your head, **on your head.**
   Put your finger on your head,
   Tell me, is it green or red?
Put your finger on your head, **on your head.**

Put your finger on your nose, **on your nose,**
Put your finger on your nose, **on your nose.**
   Put your finger on your nose,
   You can feel the cold wind blows,
Put your finger on your nose, **on your nose.**

Put your finger on your cheek, **on your cheek,**
Put your finger on your cheek, **on your cheek.**
   Put your finger on your cheek,
   Leave it there about a week,
Put your finger on your cheek, **on your cheek.**

Put your finger on your ear, **on your ear,**
Put your finger on your ear, **on your ear.**
   Put your finger on your ear,
   Leave it there about a year,
Put your finger on your ear, **on your ear.**

Put your finger on your finger, **on your finger,**
Put your finger on your finger, **on your finger.**
   Put your finger on your finger,
   And your finger on your finger,
Put your finger on your finger, **on your finger.**

In a dark, dark . . .

Children clap their own hands together then clap their partners' hands to this version of the familiar chant. At the end of the chant children pretend to stab each other, or a non-violent end is to quickly put hands behind backs, hiding the dagger.

In a dark, dark city
There's a dark, dark suburb
In the dark, dark suburb
There's a dark, dark street
In the dark, dark street
There's a dark, dark house
In the dark, dark house
There's a dark, dark room
In the dark, dark room
There's a dark, dark corner
In the dark, dark corner
There's a dark, dark cupboard
In the dark, dark cupboard
There's a dark, dark box
In the dark, dark box
There's . . . . . . a dagger

Little Sally Walker

Children are in a circle either sitting or standing. They all clap to the beat. One player sits in the middle of the circle and does the actions then chooses someone else to go into the circle.

Little Sally Walker,
Sitting in a saucer,
Crying and weeping over all
she have done.
Oh rise up on your feet,
Oh, wipe your cheeks,
Oh, turn to the east
Oh, turn to the west,
Oh, turn to the very one
that you love the best.
Now put your hand on your hip
And let your backbone slip
Shake it to the east,
Shake it to the west,
Oh, shake it to the very one
that you love the best.

Oliver Twist

Children stand in a circle chanting and doing the actions. A leader is chosen to call out the actions in the second part of the chant.

Oliver jump
Oliver jump
Oliver jump, jump, jump.

Oliver kick
Oliver kick
Oliver kick, kick, kick.

Oliver twist
Oliver twist
Oliver twist, twist, twist.

Oliver jump, jump, jump.
Oliver kick, kick, kick
Oliver twist, twist, twist.

Oliver Twist, he can't do this
So what's the use of trying?

Leader : No. 1 touch your tongue
          : No. 2 touch your shoe
          : No. 3 touch your knee
          : No. 4 touch the floor
          : No. 5 wave good-bye
          : No. 6 do the splits
All   : Good-bye Oliver Twist.

Houchi Kouchi Dance

This chant ends with the Houchi Kouchi Dance, where your bottom wiggles and your hands are tucked under your chin. Bottoms wiggle to the 4/4 beat.

Begin by finger clicking 1, 2, 3, 4.

Two clicks at the end of each line

I went down town
to the alligator farm
I sat on the fence
And the fence broke down
The alligator bit me
By the seat of the pants
And made me do
The houchi-kouchi dance
(Dance to four beats)

Three little monkeys

Divide the class into two groups.

Group 1:	Three little monkeys
	Jumping on the bed
	One fell off
All:	And broke his head.
Group 2:	Took him to the doctor,
	And the doctor said,
	'That's what you get
All:	For jumping on the bed.'

Two little monkeys... (Repeat)
One little monkey... (Repeat)

My name is Joe

Children chant the rhyme and join in with the actions.

Hi
My name is Joe
and I work in a button factory.
I have a wife and no kids.
One day my boss says to me,
'Are you busy, Joe?'
I say 'No'.
'Then push this button with your RIGHT HAND'.
(Continue pushing with your right hand as you chant)
So I did.

Hi
My name is Joe
and I work in a button factory.
I have a wife and one kid.
One day my boss says to me,
'Are you busy, Joe?'
I say 'No'.
'Then push this button with your LEFT HAND'.
(Continue pushing with both left and right hands)
So I did.

Hi
My name is Joe
and I work in a button factory.
I have a wife and two kids.
One day my boss says to me,
'Are you busy, Joe?'
I say 'No'.
'Then push this button with your RIGHT LEG'.
(Continue pushing with both hands and your right leg)
So I did.

Hi
My name is Joe
and I work in a button factory.
I have a wife and three kids.
One day my boss says to me,
'Are you busy, Joe?'
I say 'No'.
'Then push this button with your LEFT LEG'.
(Push with both legs and arms as you chant)
So I did.

Hi
My name is Joe
and I work in a button factory.
I have a wife and four kids.
One day my boss says to me
'Are you busy, Joe?'
I say 'No'.
'Then push this button with your HEAD'.
(Continue pushing with your hands, legs and head)
So I did.

Hi
My name is Joe
and I work in a button factory.
I have a wife and five kids.
One day my boss says to me,
'Are you busy, Joe?'
I say 'No'.
'Then push this button with your TONGUE'.
(Push with your hands, legs, head and tongue)
So I did.

Hi
My name is Joe
and I work in a button factory.
I have a wife and six kids.
One day my boss says to me,
'Are you busy, Joe?'
I say 'YES!'

Two-part reading

Did you feed my cow?

Group a Did you feed my cow?
Group b Did you feed my cow?
     a   Yes Mam!
     b   Will you tell me how?
     a   Yes Mam!

b Oh what did you give her?
a   Corn an' hay
b Oh what did you give her?
a   Corn an' hay.

a Did you milk her good?
b   Yes Mam!
a Did you do like you should?
b   Yes Mam!
a Oh how did you milk her?
b   Swish! Swish! Swish!
a Oh how did you milk her?
b   Swish! Swish! Swish!

a Did that cow die?
b   Yes Mam!
a With a pain in her eye?
b   Yes Mam!
a Oh how did she die?
b   Uh! Uh! Uh!
a Oh how did she die?
b   Uh! Uh! Uh!

a Did the buzzards come?
b   Yes Mam!
a For to pick her bones?
b   Yes Mam!
a Oh how did they come?
b   Flop! Flop! Flop!
a Oh how did they come?
b   Flop! Flop! Flop!

Who did? Who did?

The teacher is needed in this one.

Group 1	Who did?
Group 2	Who did?
Group 1	Who did?
Group 2	Who did?
All	Who did swallow Jo-Jo-Jo?
Group 1	Who did?
Group 2	Who did?
Group 1	Who did?
Group 2	Who did?
All	Who did swallow Jo-Jo-Jo?
Group 1	Who did?
Group 2	Who did?
Group 1	Who did?
Group 2	Who did?
Group 1	Who did swallow Jo-nah?
Group 2	Who did swallow Jo-nah?
All	Who did swallow Jo-nah down?
Group 2	Whale did
Group 1	Whale did
Group 2	Whale did
Group 1	Whale did
All	Whale did swallow Jo-Jo-Jo.
Group 2	Whale did
Group 1	Whale did
Group 2	Whale did
Group 1	Whale did
All	Whale did swallow Jo-Jo-Jo.

Group 2	**Whale did**
Group 1	**Whale did**
Group 2	**Whale did**
Group 1	**Whale did**
Group 2	**Whale did swallow Jo-nah**
Group 1	**Whale did swallow Jo-nah**
All	**Whale did swallow Jo-nah up.**

Group 1 and 2	**Gabriel**
Teacher	**Gabriel**
Group 1 and 2	**Gabriel**
Teacher	**Gabriel**
All	**Gabriel blow your trump-trump-trump.**

Group 1 and 2	**Gabriel**
Teacher	**Gabriel**
Group 1 and 2	**Gabriel**
Teacher	**Gabriel**
All	**Gabriel blow your trump-trump-trump.**

Group 1 and 2	**Gabriel**
Teacher	**Gabriel**
Group 1 and 2	**Gabriel**
Teacher	**Gabriel**
Group 1 and 2	**Gabriel blow your trum-pet**
Teacher	**Gabriel blow your trum-pet**
All	**Gabriel blow your trum-pet**

LOUD ! !

Oo-oo-ah-ah!

The class is divided in two. One group of children form a large circle and the others sit in the middle of the circle. The inner group make dreadful spooky faces as they say 'Oo-oo-ah-ah!'

A woman in a churchyard sat,
Oo-oo-ah-ah!
Very short and very fat,
Oo-oo-ah-ah!

She saw three corpses carried in,
Oo-oo-ah-ah!
Very tall and very thin,
Oo-oo-ah-ah!

Woman to the corpses said,
Oo-oo-ah-ah!
Shall I be like you when I am dead?
Oo-oo-ah-ah!

Corpses to the woman said,
Oo-oo-ah-ah!
Yes, you'll be like us when you are dead,
Oo-oo-ah-ah!
Woman to the corpses said...
(silence)

The old false leg

1   Three crows hopped on an old false leg

2   On an old false leg,

1   An old false leg,

2   Three crows sat on old false leg

All   Which lay all alone on the moor.

1   Whoever could have dropped that old false leg

2   Old false leg

1   That old false leg

2   Whoever could have dropped that old false leg

All   Out by the lake on the moor?

1   It was nobody dropped that old false leg

2   Old false leg,

1   Old false leg,

2   It was nobody dropped that old false leg,

All   Which slept out alone on the moor.

1   That old false leg jumped up on its toes

2   Up on its toes,

1   Up on its toes,

2   That old false leg jumped up on its toes

All   In the very wet mist of the moor.

1   And it hit the tail feathers off those crows

2   Off those crows,

1   Off those crows,

2   And it hit the tail feathers off those crows,

All   Caw, caw, caw, on the moor.

1   And those crows flew away quite nakedly

2   Quite nakedly

1   Quite nakedly

2   And those crows flew away quite nakedly

All   Into the mist of the moor.

1	And the false leg there upon strolled to the shore,
2	Strolled to the shore
1	Strolled to the shore
2	And the false leg there upon strolled to the shore
All	Into the lake, and was seen no more.

Put your shoes on

Individual children can read the parent or child lines or two groups of readers can read.

Parent	If you don't put your shoes on before I count fifteen then we won't go to the woods to climb the chestnut. One
Child	But I can't find them
Parent	Two
Child	I can't
Parent	They're under the sofa. Three
Child	No Oh yes
Parent	Four five six
Child	Stop — they've got knots they've got knots
Parent	You should untie the laces when you take your shoes off. Seven
Child	Will you do one shoe while I do the other then?
Parent	Eight. But that would be cheating
Child	Please
Parent	All right
Child	It always...
Parent	Nine
Child	It always sticks — I'll use my teeth.

Parent	Ten
Child	It won't it won't
	It has — look
Parent	Eleven
Child	I'm not wearing any socks
Parent	Twelve
Child	Stop counting stop counting. Mum where are my
	socks? Mum
Parent	They're in your shoes where you left them
Child	I didn't
Parent	Thirteen
Child	O they're inside out and upside down and bundled up
Parent	Fourteen
Child	Have you done the knot on the shoe you were . . .
Parent	Yes
	Put it on the right foot
Child	But socks don't have right and wrong foot
Parent	The shoes silly
	Fourteen and a half
Child	I am I am. Wait
	Don't go to the woods without me
	Look that's one shoe already
Parent	Fourteen and three-quarters
Child	There
Parent	You haven't tied the bows yet
Child	You could do them on the way there
Parent	No we won't fourteen and seven-eight
Child	Help me then
	You know I'm not fast at bows.
Parent	Fourteen and fifteen-sixteenths
Child	A single bow is all right isn't it
Parent	Fifteen. We're off
Child	See I did it
	Didn't I?

Shared reading of many parts

I am the ghost of the cave

This chant is said in a 'coming nearer voice', getting louder and louder as more and more readers join in.

1	I am the ghost of the cave
	And I'm coming to haunt you tonight.
1.2	Chris, I'm on your one step
1.2.3	Chris, I'm on your two step
1.2.3.4	Chris, I'm on your three step
1.2.3.4.5	Chris, I'm on your four step
1.2.3.4.5.6	Chris, I'm on your five step
1.2.3.4.5.6.7	Chris, I'm at your bedroom door
All	Chris, I've got you.

Father says

For this one divide the class into four groups to read quickly line by
line.

1	Father says
2	Never
3	let
4	me
1	see
2	you
3	doing
4	that
1	again
2	father says
3	tell you once
4	tell you a thousand times
1	come hell or high water
2	his finger drills my shoulder
3	never let me see you doing that again
All	my brother knows all his phrases off by heart
	so we practise them in bed at night.

Billy Batter

Divide the children into two groups.

1   Billy Batter
     What's the matter?
     How come you're so sad?
2   I lost my cat
     In the laundrymat,
     And a dragon ran off with my dad,
All My dad
     A dragon ran off with my dad!

1   Billy Batter
     What's the matter?
     How come you're so glum?
2   I ripped my jeans
     On the Coke machine,
     And a monster ran off with my mum,
All My mum
     A monster ran off with my mum!

1   Billy Batter
     Now you're better
     Happy as a tack!
2   The dragon's gone
1   to Saskatchewan;
2   The monster fell
1   In the wishing-well;
2   The cat showed up
1   With a new-born pup;
2   I fixed the rips
1   With potato chips,
All And my dad and my mum came back,
     Came back
     My dad and my mum came back!

Marsha's song

In this chant the teacher reads several lines while the children are divided into three groups.

1	Five little worms went crawling along
2	And as they went they sang this song:
All	It's RRRRRough being a worm
	It's RRRRRough as can be
3	'Cause so many things can happen to me.
Teacher	Just then a big bird came flying by
	He saw the worms and — GASP! Oh my...
1	Four little worms went crawling along
2	And as they went they sang this song:
All	It's RRRRRough being a worm
	It's RRRRRough as can be
3	'Cause so many things can happen to me.

52

Teacher	A boy on a bike went pedalling by
	He didn't see the worms and — SQUASH! Oh my...
1	Three little worms went crawling along
2	And as they went they sang this song:
All	It's RRRRRough being a worm
	It's RRRRRough as can be
3	'Cause so many things can happen to me
Teacher	A girl going fishing just came by
	She took a worm and we know why
1	Two little worms went crawling along
2	And as they went they sang this song:
All	It's RRRRRough being a worm
	It's RRRRRough as can be
3	'Cause so many things can happen to me
Teacher	A hungry chicken came pecking by
	she saw the worms and — GULP! Oh my...
1	One little worm went crawling along
2	And as he went he sang this song:
All	It's RRRRRough being a worm
	It's RRRRRough as can be
3	'Cause so many things can happen to me.
Teacher	A girl picking blackberries came this way —
	But this was really his lucky day —
	'Cause she went by
	And we know why —
All	Nobody likes worms in berry pie.

Standing on the corner

Reader 1   I was standing on the corner
Reader 2   Not doing any harm
Reader 3   Along came a policeman
Reader 4   And took me by the arm
Reader 1   He took me round the corner
Reader 2   And rang a little bell
Reader 3   Along came a police car
All   And took me to my cell.

Reader 1   I woke up in the morning
Reader 2   And looked upon the wall
Reader 3   The fleas and the bed bugs
Reader 4   Were having a game of ball
Reader 1   The score was six to nothing
Reader 2   The bedbugs were ahead.
Reader 3   The fleas hit a home run
All   And knocked me out of bed.

Alligator pie

Divide the class into six groups.

1	Alligator pie
2	Alligator pie
3	If I don't get some
4	I think I'm gonna die
5	Give away the green grass
6	give away the sky
ALL	But don't give away my alligator pie.

1	Alligator stew
2	Alligator stew
3	If I don't get some
4	I don't know what I'll do
5	Give away my furry hat,
6	give away my shoe
All	But don't give away my alligator stew.

1	Alligator soup
2	Alligator soup
3	If I don't get some
4	I think I'm gonna droop
5	Give away my hockey-stick
6	Give away my hoop
All	But don't give away my alligator soup.

I eat kids yum yum!

Divide the class into six groups.

1   A child went out one day
     She only went to play
2   A mighty monster came along
     And sang its mighty monster song.

All 'I eat kids yum yum!
     I stuff them down my tum.
     I only leave the teeth and clothes.
     (I specially like the toes)'

3   The child was not amused
     She stood there and refused.
4   Then with a skid and a little twirl
     She sang the song of a hungry girl:

All 'I eat monsters burp!
     They make me squeal and slurp
     It's time to chomp and take a chew —
     And what I'll chew is you!'

5   The monster ran like that!
     It didn't stop to chat.
6   (The child went skipping home again
     And ate her brother's model train.)

Children could invent a different ending. (The child went skipping
home... And ate...)

Pretty pear tree

This chant has eight readers with all others coming in on the chorus.
All readers come in on the **bold** print.

1   Pretty pear tree, **pretty pear tree,**
2   Way down yonder.

All **Tree in the ground,**
     The green grass growing all around and around
     The green grass growing all around.

3   And on that tree, **and on that tree**
4   There was a limb, **there was a limb**
5   The prettiest limb, **the prettiest limb**
6   I ever did see, **I ever did see**

All **Limb on the tree and the tree in the ground**
     And the green grass growing all around and around
     The green grass growing all around.

7   And on that limb, **and on that limb**
8   There was a branch, **there was a branch**
9   The prettiest branch, **the prettiest branch**
10   I ever did see, **I ever did see.**

All **Branch on the limb and the limb on the tree,**
     Tree in the ground
     And the green grass growing all around and around
     The green grass growing all around.

     And on that branch
     There was a nest . . .

And in that nest
There was an egg . . .

And on that egg
There was a bird . . .

And on that bird
There was a head . . .

And on that head
There was a hood . . .

Nonsense . . .

★★

Hello, sir

For two readers. One reads the **bold** print and the other reads the plain print.

Hello, sir. Hello, sir.
Meet you at the grocer,
No, sir. **Why, sir?**
Because I've got a cold, sir.
Where'd you get the cold, sir?
At the North Pole, sir.
How many did you catch, sir?

One, sir, two, sir, three, sir,
four, sir, five, sir, six, sir,
seven, sir, eight, sir, nine, sir, ten, sir.
All the rest were dead, sir.

How did they die, sir?
Eating applie pie, sir.
What was in the pie, sir?
A big fat fly, sir.
What was in the fly, sir?
A big fat germ, sir.
What was in the germ, sir?
A big fat you, sir.

Three little fishes

This song can be sung by everyone. Children can work out different ways to perform it but just to read the words is enough.

Down in the meddy in a itty bitty poo,
Fam fee itty fitty and a mama fitty, foo
'Fim', fed de mama fitty
'Fim if oo tan'
And day fam and day fam all over de dam.

'Top', ted de mama fitty
'Or oo ill det ost'
De fee itty fitty dinna anna be bossed.
De fee itty fitty ent off on a spwee,
And dey fam and day fam ight out to de fee.

'Wheee!' elled de itty fitties
'Ears a wot of fun,
Ee'll fim in de fee ill de day is un'.
Dey fam and dey fam and it was a wark,
Till aw aof a tudden dey taw a TARK!

'Hep', tied de itty fitties
'Dee! ook at all de fales!'
And twit as dey tood dey turned on their tails!
And bat to de poo in de meddy dey fam,
And dey fam and dey fam bat over de dam.

Boop boop dit-tem dot-tem what-tem, Chu!
Boop boop dit-tem dot-tem what-tem, Chu!
Boop boop dit-tem dot-tem what-tem, Chu!
And dey fam and dey fam bat over de dam.

The hairy toe

1   Once there was a woman went out to pick beans
2   and she found a Hairy Toe.
3   She took the Hairy Toe home with her,
4   and that night, when she went to bed,
5   the wind began to moan and groan.
6   Away off in the distance
7   she seemed to hear a voice crying

All, softly   'Where's my Hair-r-y T-o-o-oe?'

1   The woman scrooched down,
2   way under the covers
3   and about that time
4   the wind appeared to hit the house,

All	Swooosh

5	and the old house creaked and cracked
6	like something was trying to get in.
7	The voice had come nearer,
8	almost at the door now,
9	and it said,

All, louder	'Where's my Hair-r-ry To-o-oe? Who's got my Hair-r-ry To-o-oe?'

1	The woman scrooched further down
2	under the covers
3	and pulled them tight around her head.
4	The wind growled around the house
5	like some big animal
6	and r-r-r-umbled
7	over the chimbley.
8	All at once she heard the door cr-r-rack
9	and Something slipped in
10	and began to creep over the floor.
1	The floor went
2	cr-e-eak, cr-e-eak
3	at every step that thing took towards her bed.
4	The woman could almost feel it
5	bending over her bed.
6	Then in an awful voice it said:

All, getting louder	'Where's my Hair-r-ry To-o-oe? Who's got my Hair-r-ry To-o-oe? You've got it!'

The tragedy of Horathe

1   Onthe upon a time in the middle of the Thithilian
        woodth there wath a nithe little Tudor thtyle houthe.
        And in the houthe there lived a very nithe little
        family called the Ethington-Thmytheth.
        And in that family there wath

2   Grandpa Ethington-Thmythe

3   Grandma Ethington-Thmythe

4   Ma Ethington-Thmythe

5   Pa Ethington-Thmythe

6   Thither Kate Ethington-Thmythe

7   Little Thethil Ethington-Thmythe

1   One morning Pa went out hunting

2   When he came back he had with him a little bear

All   And they called him Horathe.

1   Nekth morning Pa went out hunting.
        When he came back he found there wath

3   Grandma Ethington-Thmythe

4   Ma Ethington-Thmythe

6   Thither Kate Ethington-Thmythe

7   Little Thethil Ethington-Thmythe

All   And Pa thaid

5   Where ith Grandpa?

1   And they all thaid

All   Horathe hath eaten him

1   And Pa wath mad

All   Boy wath he mad!

1   And he thaid

All   Horathe I'll thyoot you!

1   And the nekth morning Pa went out hunting
       When he came back he found there wath
4   Ma Ethington-Thymthe
6   Thither Kate Ethington-Thmythe
7   And little Thethil Ethington-Thmythe
1   And Pa thaid
5   Where ith Grandma?
1   And they all thaid

All   Horathe hath eaten her

1   And Pa wath mad

All   Boy wath he mad!

2   And he thaid

All   Horathe I'll thyoot you!

1   Nekth morning Pa went out hunting
     When he came back he found there wath
6   Thither Kate Ethington-Thmythe
7   And little Thethil Ethington-Thmythe
1   And Pa thaid
5   Where ith Ma?
1   And they both thaid

All   Horathe hath eaten her

1   And Pa wath mad

All   Boy wath he mad!

1   And he thaid Horathe I'll thyoot you!

1   And the nekth morning Pa went out hunting
     When he came back he found there wath
7   Little Thethil Ethington-Thymthe
1   And Pa thaid
5   Where ith thither Kate?
1   And little Thethil thaid

All   Horathe hath eaten her

1   And Pa wath mad

All   Boy wath he mad!

1   And he thaid

All   Horathe I'll thyoot you!

1   Nekth morning Pa went out hunting
      When he came back he found there wath only Horathe
      And Pa thaid
5   Where ith little Thethil?
1   And Horathe thaid

All   I hath eaten him

1   And Pa wath mad
All   Boy wath he mad!

1   And he thaid

All   Horathe I'll thyoot you!

      And the next morning, Horathe went out hunting . . .

Further reading

Ahlberg, Allan, *Please Mrs Butler,* Kestrel Books, London, 1983.

Bauer, Caroline Feller, *Presenting Readers Theatre,* H.W. Wilson Co., New York, 1987.

Bradman, Tony, *Poems from the Mad Family,* Blackie, London, 1987.

Chase, Richard, *American Folk Tales and Songs,* Dover Pub. Inc., New York, 1956.

Evans, P., *Jump Rope Rhymes,* The Porpoise Bookshop, San Francisco, 1955.

Dowell, Saxie, *Three Little Fishes,* Anne Rachel Music Co., New York, 1939.

Grigson, Geoffry, in C. Logue, *The Children's Book of Comic Verse,* Batsford, London, 1979.

Harrop, Beatrice, *Okki-Tokki-Unga Action Songs For Children,* A. & C. Black Ltd, London, 1976.

Jones, Bessie and Lomax Hawes, Bess, *Step It Down: Games, Plays, Songs and Stories from the Afro-American Heritage,* University of Georgia Press, Georgia, 1987.

Lee, Dennis, *Garbage Delight,* Macmillan, Canada, 1977.

Lee, Dennis, *Alligator Pie,* Houghton Mifflin Co., Canada, 1975.

Ramon, Ross, *Story Teller,* 2nd edn, Charles Merrill & Co., Ohio, 1980.

Richie, James, *The Singing Tree,* Oliver Boyd, UK, 1964.

Rosen, Michael, *Mind Your Own Business,* Andre Deutsch Ltd, London, 1974.

Taylor, Margaret (comp.), *Did You Feed My Cow?,* Thomas Y. Gowell, New York, 1956.

Turner, Ian, Factor, June and Lowenstein, W. (eds), *Cinderella Dressed in Yella,* 2nd edn, Heinemann Education Australia, Richmond, Victoria, 1978.